Woman Up!

FIVE TIPS FOR GODLY WOMEN

CATHERINE S. HAMILTON

Published by So It Is Written, LLC
Rochester, MI
SoItIsWritten.net

Woman Up! Five Tips for Godly Women
Copyright © 2025 by Catherine S. Hamilton

Edited by: So It Is Written – www.SoItIsWritten.net

Formatting: Ya Ya Ya Creative – YaYaYaCreative@gmail.com

ISBN: 979-8-9912588-4-5

LCCN: 2024926978

PRINTED AND BOUND IN THE UNITED STATES OF AMERICA

Praise & Applause for Woman Up!

"This book is a refreshing look into the God goals of womanhood! It gives brilliant biblical text to establish each tip. It is an excellent help for those who are single and/or married. We must be intentional in sharing these truths with each generation, so our futures are preserved in love, communication and sanctification. It points us back to our Father as we strive to woman up!"

–ELDER DONNA JOYNER

"At a time in my life when I realize that I have more years behind me than in front of me, this is just what I need to reflect on my experiences and become a better version of me while pleasing God first. This book is an inspirational gift to women of all ages. Her way of synthesizing these tips makes it relatable and easy to understand. Every tip is biblical, full of real-life

scenarios, and real people who make you think deeply, laugh out loud, and go to God in prayer."
–DR. JANICE JAMES KITCHINGS

"A must-read, Woman Up! *gives insight, encouragement and power to women to persevere in various trials of life. This book is a necessary conversation for 21st century women, young and old. It reminds us to live godly lives amidst so many trials and temptations in today's world. Catherine's conversation is both relevant and on point, conveying the message of how vital it is that our spiritual needs be fulfilled on a daily basis."*
–GLORIA HUFF

"This book is truly for such a time as this! I've been longing for connection and mentorship, and Woman Up! *feels like mentorship in book form. It's packed with practical tips for women of all ages and stages of life. I truly believe you'll be blessed by the wisdom it holds, especially since so much of it is grounded in Scripture. It's a resource that uplifts, empowers and points you back to God."*
–MINISTER SHOMONEIK BROWN

"There is definitely a need for women everywhere to do a self-evaluation to Woman Up! *This roadmap to success will*

encourage, inspire and challenge women to ask themselves the hard questions and help bring them closer to God! We need to uplift, motivate and help each other in love, holding each other accountable with high regard while covering our sisters in prayer. No judgement or condemnation here! Just life's lessons learned and a passion for telling others about the freedom of inviting God into your life and every situation. No matter what age you find yourself checking in at, Woman Up! *has something for you!*

-ELDER SHELIA MICHELLE JACKSON

Dedication

This book is dedicated to all women trying to live life as God intended. As we see how the world is capturing our generations, we want to do our part to partner with God as He takes back the generations of females for the kingdom.

Acknowledgements

Father God in Jesus' name by the Spirit of the Holy Ghost, I acknowledge You first. Scripture says, "Trust in the LORD with all your heart, And lean not on your own understanding; In all your ways acknowledge Him, And He shall direct your paths" (Proverbs 3:5-6 NKJV). Your Holy Spirit empowered me to write this book. Thank You for directing my path. Only You can orchestrate a seemingly happenstance meeting between a publisher and a hidden author at a conference full of thousands of people. You are amazing!

Deacon Gene Edward Hamilton, I am grateful that you are my husband. I love you. Thank you for continuing to love and support me as I am learning to *Woman Up*!

Mrs. Patricia Lawson (Momma Pat, as I like to call you), thank you for being a godly woman whose daily life, unbeknownst to you, teaches me what is good.

Tenita "Bestseller" Johnson, thank you for all you have done to guide me through the completion of writing, revising, editing, and publishing this book. The name of your company says it all: So It Is Written, LLC.

Table of Contents

Introduction

What Do You Mean, **Woman Up**?

What do you mean, *woman up?*

Women, we may see a man who should do a better job of taking care of his household and responsibilities. Instead, he abdicates his responsibilities. When we see him act all timid and neglects to take his rightful place of caregiver, provider, and protector, we say, "He needs to 'man up'!" Well, I'd like to flip the script to us women, with a play on those words and say, *"Woman up!"*

What I mean by *woman up* is to take our rightful place, based on Scripture, in exercising the character of a godly woman as we journey through this messy thing called life! It's just as important to be godly as it is important to be womanly, if not more. When we are godly, we genuinely submit to God in prayer just like Jesus did.

John Maxwell said, "Do What Jesus Did" – DWJD.[1] The only way to God is through Jesus Christ. John 14:6 (NIV) says, "Jesus answered, 'I am the way and the truth and the life. No one comes to the Father except through me." To be godly is to exhibit the character and actions that come from the indwelling Christ inside you—the reflection of Christ within you.[2] Next to that, to be womanly is to have been born with and grown into old age with the female anatomy and demeanor God created in you. Genesis 1:27 (NKJV) says, "So God created man in His *own* image; in the image of God, He created him; male and female He created them." When we are womanly, we embody maturity, care, nurturance, support, strength, excellent work ethic, sharp-wittedness, wisdom, trustworthiness, influence, submission, reliability and so much more. According to collinsdictionary.com, when a person is called womanly, it is "a term of approval, suggesting the display of traits admired by the society, such as self-possession, modesty, motherliness, and calm competence."[3] Before I go any further, I must confess that as I look back over my life up to this present moment, I fall short of so many of the character traits I just described to you! As a godly woman and as a woman in ministry, I realize I need to *woman up*!

Notice I *did not* say that *woman up* means to take our place in womanly authority because for years, I did that and caused myself to live a jacked-up life. My *ungodly, unwomanly* choices resulted in me having to work harder at living life as a single mother at the age of fifteen and later live life as a young married mother at the age of twenty-four. Honestly, those were some challenging times. Those were tough times I brought on myself.

You could say there were self-inflicted wounds resulting from taking *my womanly authority*. You know the kind of authority where I thought I was woman enough and smart enough to say whatever I wanted to say and do whatever I thought I was woman enough to do. Proverbs 12:15 (BSB) says, "The way of a fool is right in his own eyes, but a wise man listens to counsel." I tell you, just because I thought I was woman enough to say it and do it, doesn't mean it was the right thing to do.

According to Proverbs 14:12 (NIV), "There is a way that appears to be right, but in the end, it leads to death." Death? Yes, death. I am still alive today to write this book. So obviously, it wasn't physical death. However, it was a death just the same. It was death to me because I had separated myself from life in Christ with my sinful choices. There I was, engaging in married woman activities when I wasn't even a grown woman yet, much less a *married woman*! When I separated myself from living Christ's way, nothing seemed to go right! There was no physical death, but it was a death just the same because I was out of *right* relationship with the Lord Jesus Christ. My selfish, self-centered, sinful choices separated me from my relationship with the Lord Jesus.

Chil,' I thought I was in love. But I was much too young then to know what love was. In other words, I allowed my flesh to take that love thing *wayyyy* too far before the right time in life. In Song of Songs 8:4 (NLT), the writer spoke about that when he said, "Promise me, O women of Jerusalem, not to awaken love until the time is right." Without going into anymore salacious and immoral detail, I'll just say I was hard-headed. Momma used to say, "A hard head brings a soft backend (butt)!" Boy was she ever right! I was hard-headed and needed to sit my little fas' butt down somewhere! As a godly woman in ministry *now*, I realize that I still need to *woman up*! Going through the school of hard knocks like that, I learned better. And when you learn better, you do better. In this book, the whole notion of *woman up* revolves around taking our godly, womanly place of influence, Christ's way.

Translations of Titus 2:1-5 give me practical tips as I learn to *woman up*. Yes, you read right. I said, "as I learn to *woman up*." I am in process just like many of you. Nothing like the mirror of the Word that shows you yourself. Once you see yourself—I mean *really* see yourself, you must decide to continue as you are or *woman up* and make some positive changes.

Woman Up Prayer

Father, in Jesus' name by the power and the Spirit of the Holy Ghost, it is my desire to *woman up* Your way. I have not dotted every "i," nor have I crossed every "t." I want to change. I want to embody Your character. Psalm 119:33-34 (KJV) says, "Teach me, O LORD, the way of thy statutes; And I shall keep it *unto* the end. Give me understanding, and I shall keep thy law; Yea, I shall observe it with *my* whole heart." And it *is* so and so it *is* in Jesus' name. *Amen.*

(Write your own prayer in the space below.)

_____

_____

_____

_____

_____

_____

Tip #1

Communicate

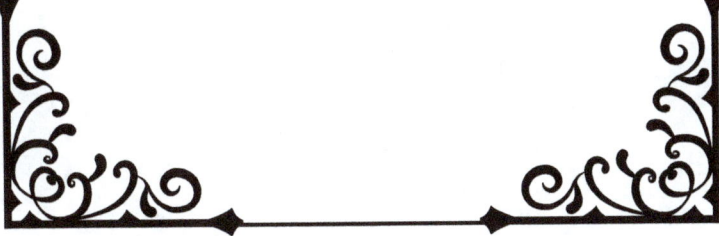

*O*ne day, I was reading and meditating on the Word of God. As I read the second chapter of Titus in The Message translation, the first verse resonated with me. Paul told Titus, "Your job is to speak out on the things that make for solid doctrine" (Titus 2:1 MSG). The Amplified translation of that same verse says it this way: "But as for you, teach the things which are in agreement with sound doctrine [which produces men and women of good character whose lifestyle identifies them as true Christians]." I thought about that for a minute. I asked myself how that verse applies to me. I thought about my own life.

See, I married a military man who is 300% military, if that's possible. Hamilton, as I call him, is a military officer, no less (retired Lieutenant Colonel Hamilton, now)! Early in our marriage, he acted as if he didn't know how to talk to me. He talked to me as if he was commanding his troops. I was not having that! We'd go toe to toe as I'd give it back to him as good as he'd given it to me. We used our mouths like guns and our words were bullets! We were not communicating. We were talking *at* one another and nothing changed. He used to make me *so* mad! Let me rephrase that. I *used to* let myself get *so* mad at him! To me, there appeared to be a double standard of him saying whatever he wanted to me, and I was supposed to only say what he thought I should say. Of course, I challenged him on that. I attempted to show him that two could play that game!

When the offense of our heated conversations remained ever present in my mind and heart, I wouldn't talk to him at all! He wanted me to shut up, so I gave him the *silent treatment* out of a mean-spirited heart. I said to myself, "Okay. You want me to shut up, I sure will!" I could be the GOAT of *silent treatment.* I wouldn't talk to him for days or even weeks! I walked through the house as if he was invisible! I am not proud to tell you that, but it's true. Truthfully, I am still growing in that area. Thank the Lord, I am much better than I used to be. I've grown to where I'm stuck in my feelings with the silent treatment only for hours instead of days or weeks. Rather than give the *silent treatment* that is mean-spirited, I use God's Word to help me keep my mouth shut until I can communicate nicely. I guess you could say I "study to be quiet and [tend to] my own business . . ." (1 Thessalonians 4:11 KJV). When love is at the center of the heart, studying to be quiet is easier. Momma used to say, "If you can't say something nice, don't say nothing at all." I like the way Berean Standard Bible says it. "When words are many, sin is unavoidable, but he who restrains his lips is wise" (Proverbs 10:19 BSB). I am grateful today that when I got to the end of my rope and cried out to God, He heard my earnest plea. He taught me His spiritual disciplines, and He taught me (and He is still teaching me) to approach the communication situation His way.

I changed.

Hamilton changed.

Thus, our situation changed. That's when we began to experience a happier home. Romans 8:28 (NKJV) says, "And we know that all things work together for good to those who love God, to those who are the called according to *His* purpose."

Over time, other hurting women conversed with me about a myriad of issues and situations. As confidential conversations increased, it came to me that I must speak out. I must speak with other women; however, not from a place of offense. I must *woman up*. I must do more than just communicate. I must communicate sound doctrine that's going to produce women of good character and matching Christian lifestyles. Then, the radio station in my head began to play, "Before I tell them, Lord please tell me."[4] When we communicate, we give or share ideas, information, and instructions with others, and we receive ideas, information, and instructions from others. Communication is important at every level, from the highest to the lowest. There's nobody higher for us to communicate with than God, our heavenly Father. First, He taught me to communicate with Him through the spiritual disciplines of reading His Word, worship through music, and praying His Word. So, get comfortable communicating with God through prayer. Then, be sure to communicate interpersonally with other women across generational lines.

Communicate with God, Through Prayer

Wayne Grudem, a noted theologian, says, "Prayer is personal communication with God."[5] I am learning to go to God first because I can't make it if I don't! When I shut down communication with God and attempt to move forward in my own knowledge and strength, I make a mess every time. For example, I had a meeting at a different school district. The first time I went, I rode with a young lady who was familiar with where we were going. She did not use a GPS. We quickly arrived at the meeting on time without incident. However, I attended the second meeting alone with a bad case of the "I've got this" syndrome. Rather than go to God in prayer for guidance and instruction on what to do, whether to use the GPS, which route to take, and when to leave, I decided I was going to travel to the meeting on my own without the aid of God or the GPS.

I had already decided I would turn onto all the roads the young lady had turned onto the week before. Needless to say, *my* plan did not work. "Many are the plans in a person's heart, but it is the LORD's purpose that prevails" (Proverbs 19:21 NIV). I will tell you that I got so lost, so confused, and so discombobulated that I finally pulled over in a panic. This is a perfect example of what happens when I lean to *my own* understanding! You best believe I went to God in prayer, *then*!

I asked Him to help me to at least get to the meeting in time to hear and participate in *some* of it. It came to me to turn around and get on the one road that was familiar, communicate with the young lady who drove us there before, and get her help. Thankfully, I arrived at the meeting thirty minutes before the meeting was over. When you go with God, you won't go wrong! He *will* direct you! No wonder the Bible says, "Seek ye first the Kingdom . . ." The Amplified translation of Scripture says it this way: "But first *and* most importantly seek (aim at, strive after) His kingdom and His righteousness [His way of doing and being right—the attitude and character of God], and all these things will be given to you also" (Matthew 6:33 AMP).

The words to Yolanda Adams' song "Before I Tell Them" came as no coincidence. Those words came to me to remind me to take my cues from God; to communicate with God; to get my guidance and instructions from God. Every time I communicate with God and follow *His* lead, everything turns out just right. I repeat. Go with God and you won't go wrong! So, *woman up* and communicate with God first through prayer. "Trust in the LORD with all your heart, And lean not unto your own understanding; In all your ways acknowledge Him, And He shall direct your paths" (Proverbs 3:5-6 NKJV). Communicate with God first through prayer because prayer changes things and prayer can change us, too.

Communicate with Other Women Across Generational Lines

Interpersonal communication simply refers to communication between people. It is never too late to *woman up* and keep the wheels of honest communication rolling between us and the women in our immediate and extended families (even church families). We must value the wisdom of our elders. When I say elders, I'm not talking about the clergy title of "elder" like Elder Sarah, Elder Donna, or Elder Shelia. I'm talking about valuing the wise counsel shared by women who may be older in life experiences than we are. I'm talking about women who will share how the Lord has taught them and brought them *through*. I'm talking about listening and learning from wise women who will genuinely pray *with* and *for* us as we seek the Lord's guidance in our daily walk.

During Women's Ministry Month 2014 at Bible Way Church of Atlas Road, Associate Pastor Willie Mae Jackson, who is the leader of Women's Ministry at our church, had Mother Janie R. Jackson and the other mothers of the church participate in a panel discussion. This discussion was open communication for women. During this panel discussion, women were able to ask relevant questions and receive honest Bible-based answers. I've never forgotten that real-talk time of communication. It was such a blessing to me!

As the mothers shared, the blessing was two-fold. First, the church mothers saw they were still needed for spiritual guidance as they lived out their Titus 2 roles. Secondly, the younger women got blessed with spiritual nuggets for life application. Older women are to strengthen and support each other as we support those who are younger. We may not always get it right, but we can all do a self-check, based on Scriptures, and see where we need to *woman up*. When *ordinary* women minister with Christian integrity, *real* women's ministry will be irresistible!

Make no mistake, immediate and extended family consists of ample women who represent our generational lineage. The freedom released when we continue honest communication with the women in our families across generational lines will do much to strengthen the family. Women living ungodly lives will be put to shame when they see our walk match our talk. All they will see is a godly and holy life. Who can argue about a holy life? When we *woman up*, we can elevate respect in the family and put womanhood back in its rightful place in the world. Proverbs 31:28 NIV says, "Her children arise and call her blessed; her husband also, and he praises her."

Keep in mind that we are communicating one way or the other by what our young girls, young adult females, and our daughters (even sons) hear us say and see us do daily. Lord, have mercy! Somebody is always listening and looking. And because they are listening and looking, we must ascribe to Matthew 5:16 (NKJV) that reminds us to "Let [our] light so shine before men, that they may see [our] good works and glorify [our] Father in heaven." So, *woman up!* Keep the lines of communication flowing and growing to avoid the alternative.

Consider the alternative:

"Look here! What goes on in this house stays in this house! Ya hear me?!"

"I don't need nobody in my business!"

"You better keep your mouth shut and keep our business to yourself!"

Perhaps you are familiar with statements like that. That kind of talk binds up or shuts down communication. It puts communication in a locked box and throws away the key! Think about family issues. In some homes, when family issues occur whether it was some type of abuse or some sort of addiction, the issue may never have been communicated and resolved! It gets swept under the rug, so to speak. You know! [Seemingly,] out of sight, out of mind!

I can look back over my own life and point out the times when I swept things under the rug. Issues may have bothered me, but I didn't dare tell anybody about them. The issues may have been out of sight (not publicly visible) for a while, but I rehearsed them in my head, and they beat so painfully in my heart. It's no wonder I stumbled over the bulging rug of thought and the gigantic lump of emotion every time I tried to walk over it. Women, so it is with our minds and hearts, too!

We may have attempted to turn a blind eye and attempted to convince ourselves that our hearts had forgotten the offense. Those issues we think we've swept away—things we've suppressed and left unchecked are bulging up out of our minds and hearts, causing us to stumble! Luke 8:17 (NIV) says, "For nothing is hidden that will not be disclosed, and nothing concealed that will not be known and brought out into the open." Whew! I've got to *woman up* and communicate interpersonally with other women across generational lines. That communication will strengthen us and help prevent us from allowing each other to suffer alone in silence.

My mind goes back to a time when the subjects we needed to talk about seemed to be taboo. They were uncomfortable to talk about. The reality of it is that some subjects or topics *were* and *still are* uncomfortable to talk about. For example, I don't remember Momma ever having *the birds and the bees* conversation with me. To add to that, I have three older sisters (Elaine, Deloris, and Geraldine) and I had a brother (Eddie, Jr.) who was oldest of all. I don't even remember a time when I got to eavesdrop on Momma having *that* conversation with any of my siblings. Just like back then, the dreaded *birds and the bees* conversation as well as so many other difficult conversations are needed in households now more than ever!

Perhaps, this only applies to me. It could be that *fear* is one of the barriers to parents, especially us women, having critical conversations with our adolescent girls and young adult females! I pause here momentarily to mention that we even fear having conversations with our sons. Some women are raising their sons alone as single mothers. Some are afraid about the *right* age at which to converse with our girls (and boys) about sensitive subjects. What's too young? Then, there is the fear of not knowing how to broach the conversations. How should a conversation like that be started? What should you say? There could be fear of not knowing how to delicately answer questions asked by our adolescent girls and young adult females (and males). Will

I know the right answers to the questions they might ask me? How must I respond to this? Lord, help us. There could also be fear of what we will find out when our adolescent girls and young adult females (and males) truthfully respond during the conversation! According to John Maxwell, "Communication is more than just sharing information. It's really about sharing yourself—your *real* self. That level of honesty is the key to being able to connect with people."[6]

Even in the midst of such valid concerns, if we would come together as godly women of influence and support each other, we might be able to overcome this fear. We would have courageous conversations with our adolescent girls and young adult females (males, too) that could positively change the trajectory of their lives. Communication through these kinds of conversations is paramount to healthy relationships across generational lines. Women, we must improve our communication and conversations between each other. Simply put, *woman up!*

Honest communication is important with the women and girls in our own families: sisters to sisters, mothers to mothers, and mothers to daughters. When we are blessed to be grandmothers, we must be available to facilitate and support the same conversations between *our* daughters and *their* daughters. We are not to communicate *for* them but support our daughters as they *woman up* to converse with their daughters. We must purposefully and intentionally be sincere with women of all ages and stages. Women will learn from the mistakes of other women and quit doing the same detrimental things over and over while expecting to get different results. Again, a reason to reach across generational lines is so our conversations and our communication can bring strength and prevent each other from suffering alone in silence. Still, the most important reason might be so that every godly woman of influence can do her part to *woman up*.

Reflection Questions

1. How often do you communicate with God during the day, and where do you communicate with Him best?

    _____

    _____

    _____

    _____

    _____

2. How often do you communicate with women in your family or friends to glean wisdom/insight?

    _____

    _____

    _____

    _____

    _____

3. Why do you think there are so many distractions to effective communication with God and other women?

_____

_____

_____

_____

_____

Woman Up Prayer

Father, in Jesus' name by the power and the Spirit of the Holy Ghost, it is my desire to *woman up* Your way. I want to engage in honest, godly communication. It's important to communicate with women, young adult females, and girls in my immediate family, extended family, as well as women worldwide. Sometimes, it's a scary thought to (as I quote Nike) "Just Do It!" But it must be done. Father, help me hide Your Scripture in my heart to push me past the fear. "For God has not given us a spirit of fear, but of power and of love and of a sound mind" (2 Timothy 1:7 NKJV). I realize that interpersonal communication across generational lines is important because "iron sharpens iron (Proverbs 27:17 NKJV). And it *is* so and so it *is* in Jesus' name. *Amen.*

(Write your own prayer on the following page.)

_____

_____

_____

_____

_____

_____

_____

_____

_____

_____

_____

_____

_____

_____

_____

_____

Tip #2

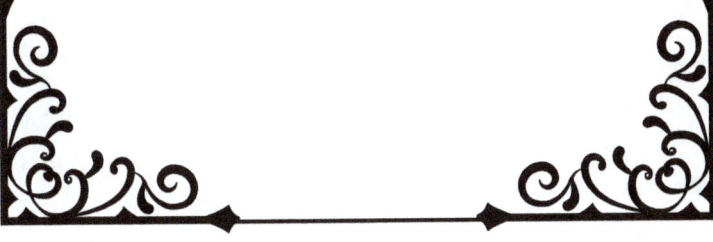

Be Reverent

My mother, Loreatha Weaver Smith, lived a reverent life. Her behavior honored God and other people. Gossiping around the house and out in the streets about other people was not her thing. Whenever someone approached her with gossip, she shook her head and I'd hear her say, "Umph, Umph, Umph!" Exodus 20:16 (NKJV) says, "You shall not bear false witness against your neighbor." So, Momma chose to be careful of what she said and how she said things. She was a *safe place* for confidential communication.

Gossiping on the telephone wasn't her thing either. Growing up, we could barely keep the phone bill paid to where any of us could talk on the phone. In fact, I only occasionally saw or heard Momma talk on the phone. She had to *woman up* and do a whole lot of other things: planting or picking something from the garden, cooking food for all the mouths she'd feed, washing clothes, working at one of the textile mills, and more. Doing so much around the house didn't leave much time for talking on the phone or gossip. She spent her time minding her own business.

Scripture in 1 Thessalonians 4:11 (NLT) says, "Make it your goal to live a quiet life, minding your own business and working with your hands, just as we instructed you before."

Reatha, as Daddy called her, was sober and sober-minded. I never saw her do any recreational drinking of any type of alcohol, let alone get drunk. I did see her taste the wine she'd make from the blackberries or muscadines we picked though. I was the youngest child and always underfoot, so she let me taste it, too. When she thought the jar of wine was ready/fermented, she poured it on the fruitcakes she made and stored them for the Christmas holidays, unless Daddy snuck in there and consumed it all. I still laugh when I think of Momma's facial expression—to unwrap the fruitcakes, reach for the jar of wine only to discover the jar empty! This godly woman had great self-control and restraint to stay sober. If it were me, I might have become a drunken lush dealing with the day-to-day challenges Daddy brought and the reality of raising five kids!

Being sober-minded, Momma thought things through and used good judgment. She remained calm in the midst of trying times and took time to do things with excellence. An example is when all my siblings and our families gathered at our parents' house one Sunday for dinner and family time. There was hardly any food to cook. I might have panicked and been wringing my hands in anxiety. Not Momma! She didn't allow herself to be sucked in by the lack of groceries. She "casted down arguments and every high thing that exalted itself against the knowledge of God, bringing every thought into captivity to the obedience of Christ" (2 Corinthians 10:5 NKJV). Not having much of anything in the fridge and pantry, Momma calmly went into the kitchen, looked at what she did have, talked to God about it, thought of a menu and prepared a meal spread that would put any all-you-can-eat restaurant to shame! Everybody ate and there was more than enough.

Momma modeled goodness. She always showed the love of God, kindness and gentleness even when I thought she shouldn't have. Every time John Doe (a pseudonym) walked miles to our house and sat in our living room all day exhibiting unstable behaviors, Momma was available to sit with him. She treated him as if he was her son. She fixed him cold glasses of water, offered him food, engaged him in calm conversation, and made sure somebody took him back home when needed. I was an angry teenager about the whole thing.

One time, I huffily asked her, "Why are you being so nice to him with his crazy self?" She responded, "You're supposed to be nice to people because you might be entertaining angels unawares."

I didn't know it then, but now I know that she answered me with the Word of God. She didn't quote book, chapter, and verse, but it was still the Word. Hebrews 13:2 (ESV) says, "Do not neglect to show hospitality to strangers, for thereby some have entertained angels unawares." Whoever showed up at our house got that same hospitality. Even Officer Shay, the highway patrol officer, who brought my brother back home after one of his early morning wrecks that totaled Daddy's car. Officer Shay got hot grits, hash and sausages, toast and jelly, and coffee. Older women must teach what is good. That teaching begins at home. Momma was a reverent woman of God who modeled goodness.

The Apostle Paul commanded Titus to teach the believing men and women of the church at Crete the behaviors they were expected to exhibit. Men's instructions are especially important for men. Since we are saved and trying to *woman up*, we will walk heavy on Paul's instructions for how *women* were to be reverent. Titus 2:3 (MSG) says, "Guide older women into lives of reverence so they end up as neither gossips nor drunks, but models of goodness." Paul told Titus to teach these things. Dr. Dharius Daniels said, "We must understand what the text meant before [we] share what it could mean."[7] Let's see what Paul meant so we can discern what it means for us now.

To be reverent is to have wholehearted respect and awe for God, respect for ourselves as godly women, and respect for others. When we are reverent, we behave and live in a way that honors God. We wear an attitude of humility and dependence on Him. In Titus 2:3 (MSG), Paul mentioned three distinct behaviors he considered characteristics of a reverent woman:

1. She is not a gossiper.

2. She is not a drunkard.

3. She is a woman who models goodness.

Be Reverent: Not a Gossiper

Paul placed importance on reverent, older women not gossiping or slandering anybody. Gossiping is telling people's business maliciously or telling lies about people. Gossiping or slandering is evil behavior because it ruins a person's good character. So, when a gossiper gossips, she is in a relationship with the evil one. Proverbs 25:9-10 (NKJV) says "Debate your case with your neighbor, And do not disclose the secret to another; Lest he who hears *it* expose your shame, And your reputation be ruined." Sometimes, gossipers call around to people as though they are doing a wellness check. Gossipers disclose private conversations with other people. For example, gossipers may say, "Hey, I was just checking on you. Is everything okay?" Once you tell the gossiper what's going on with you, the gossiper calls the next person on their unwritten, wellness checklist. "Hey, I was just checking on you today. I hope you're having a good day. I just called so-and-so. She's doing alright. She's just worried about her children. She says one of them is living an alternative lifestyle and the other one keeps bringing expensive stuff in the house, but he has no job. She is doing alright though. How are you doing?"

Refrain from gossip. God hates gossip or slander because He is the God of goodness and truth.

Sometimes, what gossipers want to broadcast is true. Just because what gossipers want to run and tell is true, doesn't mean it needs to be told. If you're wondering whether it's gossip, ask yourself the following questions. Is it honest-to-goodness truth? Is it uplifting for you to tell it? Is it building up the Kingdom and building the person up if you tell it? Asking ourselves questions like these can help us discern gossip and prompt us to end conversations before they turn into gossip. Knowing that "death and life *are* in the power of the tongue" (Proverbs 18:21 NKJV), a reverent woman of truth and prayer would not let negative, gossiping words come from her mouth.

We've got to control our gossiping tongues. Speaking of control, James 3:4-6 (NLT) says, "And a small rudder makes a huge ship turn wherever the pilot chooses to go, even though the winds are strong. In the same way, the tongue is a small thing that makes grand speeches. But a tiny spark can set a great forest on fire. And among all the parts of the body, the tongue is a flame of fire. It is an entire world of wickedness, corrupting your entire body. It can set your whole life on fire, for it is set on fire by hell itself." *Woman up* and control that tongue!

There's more than enough gossip and slander going on in the news and entertainment industry, in politics, and sometimes in our churches. Sadly, gossip goes out across all media outlets, too. Gossipers seem to have no shame and no fear of legal action against them. Additionally, gossipers proudly use the First Amendment as a license to say, write, sing, post, and share whatever they want. Gossiping is disrespectful. It compromises a person's dignity and ruins a person's reputation. It could prompt legal action against the gossiper. Avoid a gossiping woman who talks too much, tells everybody's business, stirs up wrath, and breaks up close relationships. Either way we look at it, we can't say anything and everything we want to say. Rather than a gossiper, be confidential, truthful, and speak well of others.

I see Deborah the prophet and judge as a reverent confidant who refrained from gossip (Judges 4:1-24 NKJV). While serving as Israel's judge, Deborah and Barak defeated Sisera and the Canaanite army. When Barak wouldn't lead the Israelite army against the Canaanite army unless Deborah went with him, she could have created a nasty rumor about that. However, she did not. Instead, she prophesied what would take place to Barak. She spoke well of him and spoke truthfully to him. She told him that Sisera would be defeated at the hands of a woman (Jael), and she went to battle with Barak as he requested. Carol Stine says, "Deborah lived approximately one hundred forty years after

Joshua's death. She was probably middle-aged at the time of the events described in the Book of Judges. Yet she had seen and heard enough to be a wise and respected woman whom God used in an extraordinary way."[8] Deborah refrained from gossip. She was reverent and confidential.

In my life today, Gloria H. is reverent and confidential. She discerns well and is a good judge of character. She helps without putting your business in the street. When she speaks, she gives truthful, wise counsel. Ephesians 4:15 (NLT) says, "Instead, we will speak the truth in love, growing in every way more and more like Christ, who is the head of his body, the church." Gloria H. carefully chooses her words of response. She knows "whoever guards [her] mouth preserves [her] life . . ." (Proverbs 13:3 ESV). Serving like Jesus, Gloria H. is always providing support and help for so many people. She assists and supports others without expecting anything in return. She can be trusted to help without bragging about it. When I contact her with a prayer request, I can expect results because she never hesitates to intercede on my behalf. She has gone with me to war in prayer so many times. Each time, Jesus gives the victory! In my opinion, Gloria H. is a modern-day Deborah.

I've got to *woman up* and operate in reverent confidentiality and truth. Y'all! I must do a self-check. I'm going to hold up the mirror of God's Word in front of *my own* face! It is ungodly to spread malicious gossip about people. It's ungodly to slander people. God doesn't like it. Exodus 20:16 (NKJV) says. "You shall not bear false witness against your neighbor." When my spouse, family members, friends, prayer partners, and coaching clients share with me, they must be able to discern that I will keep our conversations confidential. They must be able to trust me to speak well of them. As a godly older woman, I can do my part to walk out each day by trusting God to be the doorkeeper of my lips, keeping confidences, and speaking well of others. That is the godly thing to do.

Be Reverent: Not a Drunkard

Paul spoke of reverent women as those who were not drunkards, not addicted to wine, not heavy drinkers. It makes sense that Paul would mention not being a drunkard because the perils of overconsumption were noted in the Bible as far back as Genesis 9 when Noah consumed too much wine. No doubt, Noah would have kept his clothes on and hidden his own nakedness had he not been drunk. Galatians 5:21 (NLT) says, "envy, drunkenness, wild parties, and other sins like these. Let me tell you again, as I have before, that anyone living that sort of life will not inherit the Kingdom of God." All sin separates us from right relationship with God.

A drunken state affects total personal health. Overconsumption of alcohol impairs mental acuity. A drunkard's thoughts become confused (Proverbs 23:33 NIV). The mind becomes sick with hallucinations. Those led astray by strong drink don't behave in wisdom. They make unwise decisions. Proverbs 20:1 (NLT) says "Wine produces mockers; alcohol leads to brawls. Those led astray by drink cannot be wise." When one is boozed up, emotions can run wild from one extreme to the other. A woman who is a drunkard becomes unsteady and vulnerable to disaster (Proverbs 23:34 AMP). Other aspects of physical health become compromised by the abuse of alcohol as well. Speech becomes slurred. The eyes become bloodshot, and vision blurred. Internal organs are attacked as the alcohol "bites like a snake and poisons like a viper" (Proverbs 23:32 NIV).

Literally and practically speaking, one's drunkenness negatively affects one's relationships causing missed opportunities to show love to those who expect to have love shown. Spouse, children, extended family, friends, colleagues, and others who are opposed to overuse of alcoholic beverages avoid interactions with drunkards. One's drunkenness could also cause those in relationship with her to overindulge in alcohol and make unwise decisions themselves. A reverent woman resists causing her sister (or brother) to stumble. Scripturally, 1 Corinthians 8:12 (NLT) says, "And when you sin against other believers by encouraging them to do something they believe is wrong, you are sinning against Christ." Financially, the abuse of alcohol interferes with the appropriate execution of day-to-day household responsibilities like caring for self and others, paying bills on time, and purchasing food and medicines. Drunkenness causes poverty (Proverbs 23:21 NLT). Given all these unpleasant side effects of being a drunkard, it's best to *woman up* and stay sober.

Manoah's wife chose godly reverence and sobriety. In Judges 13:4, 7, and 14 (NKJV), a man who looked like an angel of the Lord told Manoah's wife first, then the angel told her and Manoah that she was not to drink any wine or any other fermented drink in expectation of conceiving and giving birth to a son. Samson would be that son who was appointed by God before he was even born to be a Nazirite deliverer of God's people from the Philistines. Samson's mother was obedient and reverent. Today, whether I'm an expectant mother or not (*not!*), it still literally means to refrain from overindulgence of alcoholic beverages and overindulgence of unwise decisions.

Frances is a modern-day Manoah's wife. I guess we can call her Pastor Tommy's wife! She chooses to be reverent and sober. She's not a drunkard. She makes sober-minded decisions. She keeps her temple clean to be able to pour out to others. In the Word, 1 Corinthians 3:16-17 NKJV says,

"Do you not know that you are the temple of God and *that* the Spirit of God dwells in you? If anyone defiles the temple of God, God will destroy him [her]. For the temple of God is holy, which *temple* you are." Literally, alcoholic drinks and unwise decisions are not her portion. Figuratively, though, I have seen her drunk in the Spirit. Ephesians 5:18 (NLT) says, "Don't be drunk with wine, because that will ruin your life. Instead, be filled with the Holy Spirit." Frances is filled to overflowing in the presence and power of the Holy Spirit. Frequently, she loses herself in the presence of the Holy Spirit as she worships through song, lifts her voice in effectual and fervent prayer, and preaches down a revival in the individual soul. John 4:24 (NKJV) says, "God is Spirit, and those who worship Him must worship in spirit and truth." Be somewhere in the room with Frances and get caught up in the Holy Spirit. I, joyfully, get drawn into her overflow in the Holy Spirit.

Alcoholic beverages are not my vice, but I must guard against, figuratively, being a drunkard of anything that has the potential to control and hurt and have the same harmful effects. I must not let myself get drunk from my own ego, selfishness, revenge, anger, or even unforgiveness. Self-indulgence in these five things negatively devastate the total body and relationships just the same! Ephesians 4:31-32 (NKJV) says, "Let all bitterness, wrath, anger, clamor, and evil speaking be put away from you, with all malice. And be kind to one another, tenderhearted, forgiving one another, even as God in Christ forgave you." I can think of ten seemingly positive things I must resist overindulging in, as well. I ought not overindulge in or be a drunkard of praise, food, self-love, medicine, success, money, shopping, social media, church tradition, or power, either. While all ten things are potentially *good* things, too much of a good thing is still bad for me. I choose to *woman up*. I choose to function soberly in my mind, emotions, physical and spiritual body, relationships, and finances. Being sober pleases God.

Be Reverent: Model Goodness

Paul also said reverent women model goodness. Goodness is "part of the character of God."[9] Goodness is a fruit of the Spirit: one of the good things we get from God when the Holy Spirit lives on the inside of us. Galatians 5:22-23 (NKJV) says, "But the fruit of the Spirit is love, joy, peace, longsuffering, kindness, goodness, faithfulness, gentleness, self-control. Against such there is no law." Reverent women who model goodness sacrifice themselves to do something good for others. Their sincere good works never go unnoticed. Reverent women teach what is good by what they do and say, unintentionally, as they live life day by day. They teach what is good by what they do and say, intentionally, when they make it a point to explain and show others, especially younger women, practical examples of good works.

Anna was a reverent, older woman who modeled extraordinary goodness (Luke 2:36-38, NKJV). Anna was an old prophet with a heart for God whose husband died after only seven years of marriage. Anna never remarried. She modeled for older women and young women how to walk with God as a widow. She kept only unto God after her husband died. Luke 2:37 (NKJV) says, "and this woman *was* a widow of about eighty-four years, who did not depart from the temple, but served *God* with fastings and prayers night and day." She spent all of her time worshipping in the temple. Anna modeled for older women and younger women how to put God first and how to keep worshipping and serving God no matter the circumstance or age.

Even in her old age, Anna still had her wits about her. Her life illustrated that one can still be naturally attentive and spiritually attuned to God's prompting and promises no matter how old you are. For she recognized Baby Jesus "as the long-awaited Savior and began thanking God for Him."[10] Anna was one of the first Christian missionaries to share the good news of Jesus Christ. In doing so, she modeled that God still uses older people, too! Anna lived her life on purpose. She did what she did and said what she said intentionally and unintentionally. Anna lived the epitome of reverent goodness.

In my eyes, Janice and Miriam are women who are representative of Anna today. Unlike Anna, both had their husbands with them for more than twenty and thirty years, respectively. Janice had been married for twenty-three years and ten months. Miriam had been married for thirty-three years. Neither of them matches Anna's old age, but their reverent lives of good works speak for them. As I am blessed by access to their lives, they teach what is good.

Having been left a widow far too early in life as a result of her husband passing away from cancer, Janice remains a positive, joyful woman of prayer and service to so many. Janice can be found serving her family members and friends (like me) meals that melt in your mouth. She hosts fellowship gatherings that lift the spirit. She volunteers her talents, time, and treasure at the Saron Baptist Church. She loves connecting with people and volunteering at the Lexington Medical Cancer Center-Oncology on Mondays. She makes the cancer center her temple as she interacts with the patients, prays in her heart for them, and lives the good news of Jesus in every interaction. She works as college supervisor of APEC Fellows and their mentor teachers at Columbia College. She also provides words of wisdom and professional development to educators in South Carolina school districts and internationally. "But do not forget to do good and to share, for with such sacrifices God is well pleased" (Hebrews 13:16 NKJV). This reverent woman, like Anna, teaches what is good.

Miriam was left a widow far too early in life when her husband passed away from leukemia. Still, her countenance and demeanor illustrate peace, cheerfulness, commitment to private worship, dedicated assistance to family, friends, her sorority, and the education of children. Miriam protects her peace through private worship encounters and free acts of service when she sings at various events. She gives of herself as a faithful caregiver for one of her family members. She willingly takes the initiative to jump in to supply various needs of her family members and friends. Often, it's the ministry of presence and laughter, but that good work alone is invaluable. She can be found doing sorority volunteer work at a plethora of venues. Although she is a retired teacher, Miriam's love for the educational, mental, and emotional well-being of children drives her to volunteer her skills to tutor children at Brothers and Sisters of Aiken County. She also volunteers in elementary schools to provide intervention services to children as needed. When we look at Miriam's life and all that she embodies, this reverent woman also teaches what is good.

"Let your light so shine before men, that they may see your good works and glorify your Father in heaven."
—MATTHEW 5:16 NKJV

Today, Anna's life sends a message to me. I am without excuse. As I age, there is so much I can still do to model goodness on earth as it is in heaven. I can *woman up* and surrender my will to God's will in my marriage, family, local church, and in the marketplace. I can *woman up* and share the goodness of God in how I treat people. If old-aged Anna had no complaints about arthritis, I can certainly *woman up* and enjoy the degree to which I still move about without earthly assistance. I can *woman up* and exhibit how to work and complete assignments with integrity, commitment, and excellence. I can model what is good. Titus 2:7-8 (NKJV) says, "in all things showing yourself *to be* a pattern of good works; in doctrine showing *integrity*, reverence, incorruptibility, sound speech that cannot be condemned, that one who is an opponent may be ashamed, having nothing evil to say of you." Be reverent. Be truthful and confidential. Stay sober. Teach what is good.

Reflection Questions

1. What are some other situations where gossip might be disguised as concern or care for someone and how do we differentiate between the two?

    _____

    _____

    _____

    _____

2. How does a woman's reverence for God affect her interactions with others, both within and outside the church community?

    _____

    _____

    _____

    _____

    _____

3. What challenges do you face in living out the kind of reverence Paul describes in Titus 2:3, and how can we overcome them together?

_____

_____

_____

_____

_____

Woman Up Prayer

Father, in Jesus' name by the power and the Spirit of the Holy Ghost, it is my desire to *woman up* Your way. I want to live a life of reverence that honors You. I want to speak well of You and others. Help me to be truthful and confidential because Scripture says, "And you shall know the truth, and the truth shall make you free" (John 8:32 NKJV).

Please help me to stay away from drunkenness of any earthly substance. Rather, fill me to overflowing in the Holy Ghost! Ephesians 5:18 (NKJV) says, "And do not be drunk with wine, in which is dissipation; but be filled with the Spirit." Father, I thank You for continuing to show me how to teach what is good according to Your will and not my own. I remember your powerful words of Ephesians 2:10 (NKJV) that says, "For we are His workmanship, created in Christ Jesus for good works, which God prepared beforehand that we should walk in them." Father, I walk in Your good works. And it *is* so and so it *is* in Jesus' name. *Amen.*

(Write your own prayer on the following page.)

Tip #3

Show How to Love

We have the responsibility as older women to show younger women how to love. Titus 2:4 (MSG) says, "By looking at them, the younger women will know how to love their husbands and children." Younger women and girls should be able to see our positive examples of love as they look at our daily lives. They should be inspired by how we love our husbands and children. This is not just for those of us who are already married. It's not just for those of us who have given birth to children. This tip still applies to all women.

Show How to Love Your Husband

First, if you've never been married or you're not married anymore (for whatever reason), you still have a husband. You have the perfect husband—a heavenly husband who is Jesus Christ. You don't have to settle for or be comfortable with just any earthly man. Instead of settling, choose to be spiritually selective in receiving a man who is equally yoked. Jesus will never hurt you. He will never talk to you as though you have no value or worth. He will never violate you. He will never fail to supply your needs, and He will never discourage you. He will never act out earthly jealousy towards you. He will never stop supporting you. He will never stop interceding for you before our heavenly Father, and He will never leave you. "…and lo, I am with you always, even to the end of the age. Amen" (Matthew 28:20,

NKJV). No longer do you need to look for a man. Just concentrate on getting to know and loving *the Man*! Let Jesus be your Man from Galilee! Do you know Jesus, *the Man?* Do you know how to love Him? Jesus' love language is a pure heart and quality time with Him.

Jesus, as your bridegroom and your husband, wants you to have a clean, sincere heart toward Him. Make sure you have the right motives when you speak of Him, speak to Him, and interact with Him. Jeremiah 17:9 (NKJV) says, "The heart *is* deceitful above all *things*, And desperately wicked; Who can know it?" You can be honest with yourself and Jesus concerning your heart posture. What's your sincere heart posture? Are you saying you love Jesus because you sincerely do? Or are you saying you love Jesus because you know it's a cordial thing to say and other people are saying it? You can help yourself with your heart by praying what David prayed in Psalm 51:10 (NLT) that says, "Create in me a clean heart, O God. Renew a loyal spirit within me." When you are *loyal*, your "whole being is committed to someone."[11] In being loyal to Jesus, you stay in relational harmony with who He is and adhere to His teachings.[12] Love Jesus with a pure, loyal heart.

Jesus, your husband, wants you to spend quality time with Him. He wants you to be fully present with Him. Be attentive only to Him while you're with Him. Concentrate on Him by forgetting about yourself and the billions of distractions. Forget about the bills, phone calls, your weight, social media posts, the job, and tweets. *Woman up* and engage in practical spiritual disciplines to spend time with Jesus.

Prayer is one such spiritual discipline. Simply put, prayer is communication with Him. As you communicate, you can talk to Him. But you also must quietly sit alone with Him to listen for what He has to say to you. Concerning prayer, 1 Thessalonians 5:17 (NKJV) tells you to, "Pray without ceasing." As you pray, "Be anxious for nothing, but in everything by prayer and supplication, with thanksgiving, let your requests be made known to God; and the peace of God, which surpasses all understanding, will guard your hearts and minds through Christ Jesus." (Philippians 4:6-7 NKJV).

Another spiritual discipline for spending time with Jesus is to read and meditate on Scriptures. Since Jesus is the Word (the Scriptures), every time you read and think deeply about Scriptures, you are spending time with Jesus. John 1:14 (NIV) says, "The Word became flesh and made his dwelling among us. We have seen his glory, the glory of the one and only Son, who came from the Father, full of grace and truth."

Although worship is not limited to singing, singing to Jesus in worship is a spiritual discipline. Singing to Jesus is suitable for spending quality time with Him. When you sing gospel songs, worship songs to Him that are rooted and grounded in Scriptures, you remind yourself of your love for Him and His love for you. You let the Word dwell in you. You are honoring Him and putting your focus on Him. Part of Ephesians 5:19 (NIV) says, "Sing and make music from your heart to the Lord."

Let your genuine life show this to younger women who have no earthly husband so they can be secure in their relationship with Jesus. The New Living Translation of Titus 2:4 says, "These older women must train the younger women to love their husbands. . ." Train means "to teach and form by practice."[13] Practice loving Jesus as your husband. Falling in love with Jesus, loving Jesus, and spending time with Him is the best thing any woman has ever done!

Secondly, for those of us who are married, we are to love Jesus first and spend quality time with Him, too. Then, we are to love and show how to love our earthly husbands. We are to show younger women how we love our husbands God's way. As they watch us go about our daily lives, young women ought to be able to see great positive examples.

I confess that I am still growing in this area. As I *woman up*, I am learning that loving my husband means a whole lot more than saying, "I love you" and giving him a kiss when he goes off to work in the mornings. I am learning that loving him means studying him to get to know what he likes so I can do what he likes (and not do what he doesn't like). *Caveat: We are to keep studying our husbands until death do us part because, as people, we change as we grow.*

A clean, pure heart is attractive to my earthly husband, too. I am learning to show Hamilton that I love him by continuing to keep myself attractive to and for Him. The Word in 1 Peter 3:3-4 (NKJV) says, "Do not let your adornment be *merely* outward—arranging the hair, wearing gold, or putting on *fine* apparel—rather *let it be* the hidden person of the heart, with the incorruptible *beauty* of a gentle and quiet spirit, which is very precious in the sight of God." When I do this, I'm dressed more in what my husband likes than at any other time. The International Children's Bible (ICB) translation says it this way: "It is not fancy hair, gold jewelry, or fine clothes that should make you beautiful. No, your beauty should come from within you—the beauty of a gentle and quiet spirit. This beauty will never disappear, and it is worth very much to God."

Not only am I making sure I look attractive *to him* and *for him*, but I am also learning to *help him* look attractive *to me* by cooking and preparing healthy meals. I want to keep his (and my) cholesterol levels, blood sugar levels, and blood pressure levels stable and healthy. I am learning to walk two miles with him and dance with him at home for exercise. The Word in 1 Corinthians 6:19-20 (KJV) says, "What?

know ye not that your body is the temple of the Holy Ghost *which is* in you, which ye have of God, and ye are not your own? For ye are bought with a price: therefore glorify God in your body, and in your spirit, which are God's."

I am learning to show him that I love and respect him by acknowledging his leadership role in our home. "God has assigned the responsibility of spiritual leadership in the home to husbands."[14] Ephesians 5:23 (NKJV) says, "For the husband is head of the wife, as also Christ is head of the church; and He is the Savior of the body." As Hamilton leads, things don't always go as he intends. When I feel his leadership didn't go as he planned, I am learning to pray for him. Many times, I wear myself out supporting him and encouraging his growth in leadership. John C. Maxwell says, "Everyone deserves to be led well."[15] I try to help my husband lead well.

I am still learning to show him that I love him by discussing major decisions with him as I respect his role as the head of our home. That hasn't been easy because I was used to making my own decisions for my daughter and myself before we married. When we married, he and I came together as one. I am trying to *woman up* because Ephesians 5:22 (NKJV) says, "Wives, submit to your own husbands, as to the Lord." For example, I was offered a part-time job opportunity. I considered taking the job, depending upon his demeanor and response. We discussed this opportunity. Based on his pros and cons during our discussion, I declined the opportunity.

Sometimes, we have disagreements, or he does something that makes no sense to me. (For the record, I am positive I do things that make no sense to him, as well!) I am learning to *woman up*. I show him how much I love him by forgiving him quicker than in the past. "Bear with each other and forgive one another if any of you has a grievance against someone. Forgive as the Lord forgave you" is what Colossians 3:13 (NIV) says. I can't lie. I must stay on top of myself about this one, too. The Scriptures bring me back in line!

When Hamilton does something that makes me want to kick him in the teeth, I used to give him the silent treatment for days and weeks. I knew he couldn't take me giving him the silent treatment. I did it to punish him for hurting my feelings and to manipulate him into working hard to get "out of the doghouse" with me. Then I learned that manipulation is the heart of witchcraft. I was behaving like a witch. Manipulation utilizes the power of the flesh rather than trusting in the Lord's power. Manipulation tries to force another person to do what he or she would not normally do. Manipulation could even pretend to be kind and good, helpful and trustworthy while, at the same time, having the hidden motive of increasing the chances of getting what you want. Manipulation is a sin.

Galatians 5:19-21 (NIV) says, "The acts of the flesh are obvious: sexual immorality, impurity and debauchery; idolatry and witchcraft; hatred, discord, jealousy, fits of rage, selfish ambition, dissensions, factions and envy; drunkenness, orgies, and the like. I warn you, as I did before, that those who live like this will not inherit the kingdom of God." The Word of God convicted my heart. I confessed to God, repented, and accepted the Lord's forgiveness. So, what it comes down to is our heart's allegiance. Well, is my heart's allegiance to my husband or my flesh? I had to *woman up*! If I can pledge allegiance to the flag, above that I pledge allegiance to God and my husband.

You've got to *woman up*, too. If you find that you have manipulated your husband or you are tempted to manipulate him, the best thing to do is step back and get alone with Jesus in the Scriptures. Our righteousness is in Him. When we seek Him, He teaches us the compassion we need to put our husbands before ourselves. Then, manipulation has no power over us.

That's a lot of work, and I haven't even gotten to the work of mothering yet. That just goes to show us that our husbands ought to take priority over our children. Do some research on God's biblical order. You'll see. God's order builds *strong* marriages and cuts down on the divorce rate. Ephesians 5:24 (NIV) says, "Now as the church submits to Christ, so also wives should submit to their husbands in everything." The word *submit* used to send me into a tailspin. I fought against it and jumped on the feminist bandwagon—until the Holy Spirit taught me God's way based on God's Word in Genesis 3:16 NIV. Scripture says, "To the woman he said, 'I will make your pains in childbearing very severe; with painful labor you will give birth to children. Your desire will be for your husband, and he will rule over you.'"

The word *everything* made my brow furrow, too. I sarcastically questioned God, "In everything? What about when he wants to 'be fruitful and multiply' and I, occasionally, feel too tired for that?" The answer came to me as 1 Corinthians 7:3-5 (NIV): "The husband should fulfill his marital duty to his wife, and likewise the wife to her husband. The wife does not have authority over her own body but yields it to her husband. In the same way, the husband does not have authority over his own body but yields it to his wife. Do not deprive each other except perhaps by mutual consent and for a time, so that you may devote yourselves to prayer. Then come together again so that Satan will not tempt you because of your lack of self-control." That passage of Scripture taught me that in a loving marriage, the spouses will agree in a situation like that as they, "Submit to one another out of reverence for Christ" (Ephesians 5:21 NIV). I learned to *woman up*.

Right now, you may be thinking, "Cat, you must be crazy! Do you expect me to do all of that when my husband is passionately wrong in so many areas? He just won't try to live right!" Listen! I get it! I understand! *I* don't expect you to do *anything. The Lord wants us to do all of that!* Growing up, I heard this quote: "A good wife can bring a no-good man in." That was a paraphrase of 1 Peter 3:1 (NKJV) which says, "Wives, likewise, *be* submissive to your own husbands, that even if some do not obey the word, they, without a word, may be won by the conduct of their wives." Just know that *what we do and how we do it* as godly women of influence really matters. *Woman up* to live upright before the Lord. The Lord is well able to oversee the rest.

Lord knows, I pray *with* my husband. Certainly, I pray for him, too. I pray for him to take and keep his rightful place in relationship with God. I pray for him to keep his rightful place as head of our home and marriage, in our family, and his godly place in society.

Show How To Love Your Children

Based on Titus 2:4 NLT, we have the responsibility as older women to show younger women how to love their children as well. "Children are a blessing and a gift from the

LORD. Having a lot of children to take care of you in your old age is like a warrior with a lot of arrows" (Psalm 127:3-4 CEV). Women don't have to birth children physically in order to show how to love children or to teach children how to love others. We need only to think about the time when we were children. Think of how we were loved by our parents and female caretakers. Think of how we needed to be cared for and were cared for by mother figures when our mothers were unable to do so. Many mother figures filled the void. Nowadays, we can even Google how to show younger women how to show love to their children. We are without excuse.

I do want to share a bit of my motherly learning. When my children were little, I showed them how I loved them by sharing the Word with them in subtle ways. I read Scripture to them and with them. I prayed for them and with them. I provided the things they needed and some of what they wanted. I disciplined them firmly and fairly. Yes, ma'am! I whipped butt 'round here! It's not going to hurt them when it's done in love. "Spare the rod, spoil the child" is how it's often quoted. However, Proverbs 13:24 (NLT) says, "Those who spare the rod of discipline hate their children. Those who love their children care enough to discipline them." *Woman up* and discipline your children as God leads you.

The politically correct way to say it is they got spankings, sent to time out, got grounded, and lost privileges. To do that, I had to be home with them as much as possible. I did not pass them off on to other people, from pillar to post (as my mom used to say) every weekend!

I loved my two children enough to make some unpopular decisions in their eyes. I had to *woman up* and decline a lot of things they wanted me to agree with. I didn't co-sign on behaviors that were detrimental to their physical, emotional, mental, financial, relational, or spiritual health. Of course, that didn't sit well with them. I had to love them enough to serve in the parental role I was assigned rather than abdicate my responsibilities in order to be liked by them as a friend.

One time, Esha said, "Can't you just be a regular mom and listen and go along with it?"

I said, "I'm not a regular mom. I'm *your* mom, and I've got to say what the Word of God says about it."

There was a time when Edwin wanted to be the *head of the household* while his dad was away on military duty. He took that saying literally rather than the way it was spoken figuratively. He thought he could tell me what to do. You already know *exactly* how that turned out!

In doing the work of loving my children and showing them how to love, I got the opportunity to observe them. I got the opportunity to notice their gifts and talents. I got the opportunity to attempt to guide and encourage Esha and Edwin into using their gifts and talents for the Lord's service, not the world's. I had to realize that their gifts and talents were not only to be used within the four walls of a physical church. They were to also be used out in the marketplace to serve the body of Christ wherever they find themselves. That was quite a job, but it was my responsibility and privilege as a mother and a godly woman. It was worth it!

Now, I am still learning to show Esha and Edwin how to love their children even as they have grown into beautifully grounded adults. Esha loves everybody's children as though they are her very own. Edwin has three children. Watching him and Ajaree' with Abigail, Edwin Jaylen, and Ariah affords me the opportunity to see them love their children and show their children how to love. It blesses me to see the extent to which my parental training has touched their lives.

Reflection Questions

1. Why is it important to be spiritually selective in relationships, especially in choosing a spouse?

_____

_____

_____

_____

_____

2. How does the example of Jesus as a "perfect husband" shape your view of earthly relationships?

_____

_____

_____

_____

_____

3. In what ways can older women model love and faithfulness to younger women, even if they are not married or do not have children?

_____

_____

_____

_____

_____

_____

4. The author talks about learning from mistakes and growing in love and submission. In what areas of your life do you need to **woman up** and commit to growing in Christ-like love?

_____

_____

_____

_____

_____

_____

Woman Up Prayer

Father, in Jesus' name by the power and the Spirit of the Holy Ghost, it is my desire to *woman up* Your way. I want to love my husband and children infinitely and unconditionally. Help me to love and support them all. Guide me to chastise the children as you ordained. I want to show younger women how to love their husbands and children. Scripture in 1 Corinthians 16:14 (NKJV) says, "Let all *that* you *do* be done with love." Oh God, help me instruct younger women in accordance with Your Word. Do it, Lord. And it *is* so and so it *is* in Jesus' name. *Amen.*

(Write your own prayer in the space below.)

_____

_____

_____

_____

_____

Tip #4

Show How to Love More

*P*aul pointed out to Titus a few more specific ways older women must show younger women how to love their husbands and children. Titus 2:5 (MSG) says, "Be virtuous and pure, keep a good house, be good wives. We don't want anyone looking down on God's Message because of their behavior." The way that reads sounds like it should be easily understood, but other translations use more specific words. The New King James Version says, "*to be* discreet, chaste, homemakers, good, obedient to their own husbands, that the word of God may not be blasphemed." Either way the translations state it, we must understand what the verse meant (or certain words meant) and uncover what that verse means, practically, for us today. In considering what it could look like for us today, we unpack certain words like discreet, chaste, homemakers, and blasphemed. We are better able to envision instances of life application for us, in the now, when we understand these words.

Be Discreet

The Apostle Paul tells Titus to teach the older women to show their husbands and children love by being discreet. Discreet means to think, feel, speak, and behave appropriately as a believer; to be "of sound mind and self-controlled."[16] When we are discreet, unmarried and married older women discern potential hazards and use caution to avoid errors and lapses in judgment. For me, doing what is appropriate is avoiding extremes like wearing clothes so tight that I need a bottle of oil to slide them on and a crowbar to take them off. I avoid wearing low-cut tops to where my breasts are seen before anybody can see the rest of me.

In 1 Timothy 2:9 (NLT), it says, "And I want women to be modest in their appearance. They should wear decent and appropriate clothing and not draw attention to themselves by the way they fix their hair or by wearing gold or pearls or expensive clothes." Just because a store sells trendy inappropriate clothing doesn't mean I should buy those clothes or wear them if they are inappropriate for me. Proverbs 31:25 (NKJV) says, "Strength and honor are her clothing. She shall rejoice in time to come." Those are the kinds of clothes I want to wear. Believing women are discreet and they teach younger women how to love their husbands and children by being discreet.

Be Chaste

Titus was to teach the older women to show younger women how to love their (husbands and) children by being chaste. Chaste means sexually undefiled; "to not have sex with anyone, or to only have sex with your own husband or wife [for men]."[17] Chaste also means to be pure and clean and undefiled in devotion to Jesus, in thought and desire, in language, or conversations.

In other words, we are to keep our minds, mouths, and bodies pure. Although chastity is usually relegated to sexual acts, godly women use the word of God to chase lewd thoughts from our minds. Godly women use the Word of God to keep filthy, vulgar jokes and other gossipy conversation from our mouths. A helpful Scripture is "The temptations in your life are no different from what others experience. And God is faithful. He will not allow the temptation to be more than you can stand. When you are tempted, he will show you a way out so that you can endure." (1 Corinthians 10:13 NLT).

Older unmarried women of God must show our children how to love by living and teaching younger women how to refrain from the trap of *making out or petting*. Those are terms that mean "touching each other inappropriately and getting the *motors of passion running*, which is only to be saved for the marriage bed."[18] While one might think *making out or petting* is fun, it can easily get out of hand. *Woman up* and teach young women how to set boundaries for themselves. Encourage them to protect those boundaries no matter how reassuring the smooth talker *appears* to be! Teach the younger women to use restraint and insist on purity throughout the relationship until marriage. The words of 2 Timothy 2:22 (NKJV) says, "Flee also youthful lusts; but pursue righteousness, faith, love, peace with those who call on the Lord out of a pure heart."

Being careful of the company we keep is another boundary to set. "Do not be misled: 'Bad company corrupts good character'" (1 Corinthians 15:33 NIV). Avoid hanging around older women who encourage inappropriate behaviors. For example, avoid hanging around older women who brag, "I'm a cougar, honey! Rrrhhhrr!" The cougar I am referring to is an older woman who is always on the hunt to have inappropriate relationships with much younger males. Clearly, age is not the issue here since love knows no age limits. The issue is the hunt for the ungodly relationship and the bragging, since such behavior is hardly anything that should be bragged about. The behavior is a red flag that could be an indication of a risky character flaw.

More than anything else, unmarried women must refrain from laying on your backs with your legs positioned at ten minutes to two, like hands on a clock. Keep your legs closed! Protect your body! Keep your body clean and pure. "It is God's will that you should be sanctified: that you should avoid sexual immorality; that each of you should learn to control your own body in a way that is holy and honorable," (1 Thessalonians 4:3-4 NIV). We can learn based off the experiences and wise words of others. Or we can be forced to learn our lessons the hard way when life happens to us. Receive these words of wisdom from me— somebody who wishes she would not have had to learn lessons the hard way.

Avoid physical intimacy before marriage. It invites ungodly connections that cling to your life even after they are physically gone. When you unite with somebody, or a lot of bodies, you become one with that person/those persons. Be mindful and keep that type of intimacy sacred for marriage.

As an older married woman, I can speak from experience. I've got to be chaste. I stick with *my own* husband. I am devoted to *my* husband. I do that by considering a lot of things that could have the potential to violate marriage chastity. As an older woman who is responsible for showing younger women how to love their husbands (and children), I model being cordial and respectful around other men. I'm not grinning and skinning in their faces. Believe me. It matters.

Ephesians 5:33 (NKJV) says, "Nevertheless let each one of you in particular so love his own wife as himself, and let the wife *see* that she respects *her* husband." Live a lifestyle of respect. I block flirtatious conversation. I *woman up* and carry myself with respect. Then, I receive respect in return. I avoid inappropriate contact. That cuts down on the possibility of inviting inappropriate thoughts and fantasies. Even when I serve at church, I respond with quick side hugs or a quick pat on the shoulder when encountering males. Something as simple as that goes a long way toward reducing the tendency for lewd and lascivious imaginations.

Scripture is clear regarding adultery! Exodus 20:14 (KJV) says, "Thou shalt not commit adultery." The writer of Hebrews had something to say about marriage and adultery as well. "Let marriage be held in honor among all, and let the marriage bed be undefiled, for God will judge the sexually immoral and adulterous" (Hebrews 13:4 ESV). I keep the marriage bed for *my own* husband. I leave everybody else's husband alone. I remain chaste and faithful to *my* husband in body and in mind. He and I are one. "… The two will become one flesh" (1 Corinthians 6:16 NIV). Godly women, certainly married women, are chaste.

Be a Homemaker

Paul told Titus to teach the older women how to love their husbands and children by being homemakers. A homemaker is someone who builds and establishes a God-honored home. Homemakers "keep house and make sure things run smoothly there (whether they work outside the home or not)."[19] Proverbs 14:1 (NKJV) says, "The wise woman builds her house, but the foolish pulls it down with her hands." I am wise and still learning to *woman up* to be a good homemaker. When I worked outside the home for thirty years of our marriage, I still took care of our home and kept things running smoothly in the house just like I do in our retired years now.

Proverbs 24:3 (NKJV) says, "Through wisdom a house is built, And by understanding it is established." I learned early on that Hamilton is a penny pincher. He's a tightwad. Don't tell him I told you! To put that another way, he is good at saving for us to live comfortably. He and I came from humble beginnings. So, extravagance is not an option. I show how to love him by living within our means. Instead of wanting a bigger house, I show him I love him by concentrating on making the little brick house we do have into a home where God rules and reigns.

A portion of Psalm 127:1 (KJV) says, "Except the LORD build the house, They labor in vain that build it." I read and meditate on Scripture in our home. We discuss Scripture and I live it as best I can here. I constantly pray and thank the Lord in our home. Praise and worship through song floats around in our home. Family time and laughter resides here. Peace settles here. This is a comfortable and safe place to be. When you walk into our home, I am inviting you to walk into the joy of the Lord that a homemaker has co-labored with the Lord to create.

Some people attach a negative connotation to being a homemaker, but I count it a privilege and an honor. Check your perspective concerning the role of a homemaker. I let no one taint that perspective for me. I show my husband

and children how to love by engaging in the hard, fulfilling work of being a homemaker.

As a married homemaker, even when I worked outside the home daily, I still served as wife to my husband and mother to our children. Some days were challenging, but I was not alone. I was able to do it by the help of the Lord. I "lifted mine eyes unto the hills, from whence cometh my help because I knew [all] my help cometh from the LORD, which made heaven and earth" (Psalm 121:1-2 KJV). I kept the house clean. I kept food on the table. I kept clothes washed, dried, and folded. I checked our children's homework. I helped with projects. I got the children to color guard/flag core practice, to the soccer field, and to the band concerts on time. I read aloud to them. I made sure everybody had a bath, said prayers, and was in bed to get a good night's rest for the next day. After the house was quiet, I stayed up later to perfect lesson plans, prepare for professional development presentations, and wind down in worship before snuggling up to "The Mr." and getting a little sleep for myself. *It is* possible to be a married homemaker and work outside the home.

I am retired and at home now. Our children are all grown up and living in their own homes. One of our children has children of his own. Yet, I continue to be a married homemaker who works in the home. I still make sure everything runs smoothly. I invite and welcome the Lord into our home every day. Everything is clean and kept up. There is always plenty to eat on the table. Our children and their family, as well as friends, come over for visits to enjoy the atmosphere and fellowship that I've been blessed to create as a homemaker. Being a homemaker wasn't easy then, and it is not easy now. No matter if you are old or young, unmarried or married, work outside the home or work within the home. If you have a home, you have the responsibility to be a homemaker who establishes a God-honored home. You should be a homemaker who cherishes home and family. "My people will live in peaceful dwelling places, in secure homes, in undisturbed places of rest" (Isaiah 32:18 NIV).

Be Good and Do Good

Paul told Titus to teach the older women how to love their husbands and children by being good or doing good. Showing hospitality is good. Kindness and friendliness to family, strangers, visitors, former colleagues, guests, and clients really matter. Extending generosity is good. I sacrifice to give time, materials and possessions, wisdom and knowledge, and energy to others. Many people lack kindness, civility, and common courtesy today. It seems that having a nasty attitude and being "messy" to figuratively cause chaos and calamity is celebrated all over the news

these days. I am called to *woman up* and be a model of
kindness and self-less love, hospitality, and generosity to my
fellowman. Romans 12:13 (NIV) says, "Share with the
Lord's people who are in need. Practice hospitality." Show
how to love by being good and doing good.

Be Obedient and Submissive

Paul told Titus to teach the older women how to love
their husbands and children by being obedient to their own
husbands. Titus 2:5 (NKJV) says, "*to be* discreet, chaste,
homemakers, good, *obedient* to their own husbands, that the
word of God may not be blasphemed." Some translations
say, ". . . submissive to their husbands." For example, Titus
2:5 (NLT) says, "to live wisely and be pure, to work in their
homes, to do good, and to be submissive to their husbands.
Then they will not bring shame on the word of God."
According to Dr. J. Vernon McGee, obedient means
respond.[20] Wives are to *respond to* our husbands since
husbands/men are the initiators. A funny example to
illustrate that charge from Dr. McGee was, "No woman
should say I love you to a man until after he says it first.
Once your husband tells you he loves you, then tell him you
love him back in response."[21] Ephesians 5:21 (NIV) says,
"Submit to one another out of reverence for Christ."

When it comes to my husband, the words *obey* and
submit, or any derivative thereof, used to send me into a

tailspin. For somebody today, "Them's fightin' words!" as Bugs Bunny says to Yosemite Sam.[22] I used to fight against those two words until the Holy Spirit taught me to study the words considering how Jesus lived them out.

In that sense, being obedient refers to being obligated to do something unwillingly or willingly whenever we are under authority. Even Jesus, in all His power and authority, was obedient. There were times when Jesus was obedient to God the Father when He did what God told Him to do. Immediately, my mind goes to God's plan for Jesus to die on the cross for the sin of the world. Jesus obeyed that plan because that was God's way to redeem humankind. Philippians 2:8 (NIV) says, "And being found in appearance as a man, he humbled himself by becoming obedient to death—even death on a cross!" There were also times when Jesus did not do anything if God had not told Him to do it. In Matthew 13:54-58 (NIV), Jesus went back to His hometown. While He was there teaching, the people didn't believe in what He taught or His miraculous powers because they remembered who His earthly parents and siblings were. Verse 58 says, "And he did not do many miracles there because of their lack of faith." God, the Father, did not tell Jesus to do many miracles and Jesus did not do many. He only performed a few miracles.

I am obligated to be obedient to my husband. He is the authority in our home, and he is the head of our house. For example, we were scheduled to go out of town. Since my "Maintenance Required" light in the car was due to come on any day, Hamilton told me to keep calling the Toyota store until they found an appointment to fit the car in for its service. Reluctantly, I called to inquire about a car appointment for two days in a row and several times on that Thursday. By that Thursday afternoon, a representative from Toyota called me to bring the car. The car was serviced and ready for our trip to Florida! "But I want you to realize that the head of every man is Christ, and the head of the woman is man, and the head of Christ is God" (1 Corinthians 11:3 NIV). Another example is when Hamilton planned to get a specific security system. His system of choice was not the choice I would have made, but I did not interfere with the process. He purchased the security system. When the security installer came, I followed Hamilton's instructions. He had the system set up so he could monitor it and shared it with me. Now, we have extra protection.

Considering Jesus' life, being submissive refers to abiding by someone else's wishes with a ready attitude and spirit. A well-known account of Jesus being submissive to the will of God the Father is found in the book of Matthew 26:36-46 (NIV). It was time for Jesus' betrayal and arrest. Jesus and the disciples were in the garden of Gethsemane, where

He told the disciples to stay and watch as He went farther to pray. Three times, Jesus asked God the Father, "My Father, if it is possible, may this cup be taken from me. Yet not as I will, but as You will" (Matthew 26:39 NIV). When Jesus returned to His disciples and found them sleeping, He chastised them and went back to pray again saying, "My Father, if it is not possible for this cup to be taken away unless I drink it, may your will be done" (Matthew 26:42 NIV). He went back to the disciples and found them sleeping again. So, He left them to go pray the same thing for the third time. By the time Jesus' betrayer got to Him, His mind was made up, He was ready, and He was submissive to God the Father. "Look, the hour has come, and the Son of Man is delivered into the hands of sinners" (Matthew 26:45 NIV).

> *"Wives, submit yourselves to your husbands,*
> *as is fitting in the Lord."*
> –COLOSSIANS 3:18 NIV

Like Jesus decided, I *decide* to be submissive to Hamilton's wishes with a ready attitude and spirit. One Saturday, it seemed like the perfect day to get some things done in the house and get in a little uninterrupted writing. However, Hamilton wanted me to accompany him to a funeral in the morning and a wedding that evening in a country town two and a half hours away. Although what *I* wanted to do was on my radar, I had gotten started on my to-do list Friday evening and made some headway on my tasks. That Saturday, I chose to *woman up*! I made up my mind, got dressed and tenderly hung out with my husband. I was submissive to him to attend events that were really important to him.

Show Reverence to God: No Blasphemy

Titus 2:5 NKJV teaches us to live in such a way that God is not blasphemed. Blaspheme means to write or "speak with contempt about God or to be defiantly irreverent; to reproach God's name, character, work, or attributes."[23] I don't want to blaspheme God in the way I act, either. When I say I identify myself as a believer, as a Christian, as a godly woman, it is expected that my daily actions portray the same. I realize I do "damage to the Christian testimony"[24] when I say I am a Christian but act the opposite. When we say one thing and do another, we are lying to ourselves, to God, and to all. We taint our witness and negate our credibility to teach others spiritual principles. Romans 14:16 (KJV) says, "Let not then your good be evil spoken of." Since I represent God through Christ Jesus, younger women (and everybody else) expect to see me do what Jesus did, so to speak. Doing what is contrary to what Jesus would do disrespects and insults God. Instead of blaspheming God, always give Him the reverence He deserves.

Titus was assigned (by Paul) to teach what is proper (appropriate, correct). Titus was to teach sound doctrine (teaching that rightly explains what God has revealed to us in His Word). Never mind what itching ears of the world want to hear. In other words, never mind teaching what is popular; what everybody else is doing. *Woman up* and teach what needs to be heard and seen to make the world better.

Reflection Questions

1. What does it mean to be "discreet" in the context of loving one's husband and children?

    _____

    _____

    _____

    _____

    _____

2. Why is it important for an older woman to reflect love for her family?

    _____

    _____

    _____

    _____

    _____

    _____

3. How does the author suggest women can create a
   God-honored home?

   _____

   _____

   _____

   _____

   _____

   _____

Woman Up Prayer

Father, in Jesus' name by the power and the Spirit of the Holy Ghost, it is my desire to *woman up* Your way. I want my life to be a good example of purity. I want to teach the younger women how to keep a good house and be a good wife to their own husbands. Let the ministry of my marriage and the joy of my mothering be an encouragement to all women for how to build their own God-honored home in every way. For I know, "Except the LORD build the house, they labor in vain that build it" (Psalm 127:1 KJV). Lord, I am in Your hands. And it *is* so and so it *is* in Jesus' name. *Amen.*

(Write your own prayer in the space below.)

_____

_____

_____

_____

_____

_____

Tip #5

Chase Him and Receive the Wise Teaching

In learning to *woman up*, every woman has a role to play. We are all responsible for checking ourselves and supporting each other across generational lines. Younger women have great responsibility in all of this, too. Younger women must do at least two things: chase after a relationship with Jesus Christ first and seek sage instruction from older women. Younger women can receive and apply that instruction as an unintentional teaching by watching the very life of a godly older woman. Younger women can also glean intentionally from conversations and interactions with older godly women.

Chase After Jesus

Younger women must constantly chase after a deeper relationship with the Lord Jesus. He loves you. He came from heaven to earth so you can have life and have it to the fullest. In John 10:10 (NKJV), Jesus said out of His own mouth, "The thief does not come except to steal, and to kill, and to destroy. I have come that they may have life, and that they may have it more abundantly." He is for you! He paid the hefty price on Calvary's cross for your sins as evidence of His unconditional and infinite love for you.

I realize that I am instructing you to do something different from what many peers tell you, especially if you're unmarried. Many times, your peers will tell you to focus on nabbing a husband. They'll encourage you to get yourself all "dolled up." They'll encourage you to dress provocatively to get noticed and go hunting for your "Boaz." They might even go shopping with you and hang out with you as you get dressed. They might encourage you to put on more makeup than a funeral director uses on a dead person. Your peers may help you put on false lashes that are so long, thick and heavy that you need Velcro to hold your eyes open. They may encourage you to paint your lips with fire truck-red lipstick, put in hair weave that extends from the top of your head down to your knees, and put on a lowcut blouse that exposes your breasts more than it covers them. Some may even encourage you to put on a sheer short and tight skirt and rock a pair of five-inch heels in order to find your Boaz! Dressed like that, you'll probably find Buzzard or Bozo! I highly doubt you'll find a man like Boaz!

In the Bible, young Ruth sought to live life as a godly single woman after her husband died. She spent her time caring for Naomi and getting to know Naomi's God. Ruth spent time working hard out in the fields to better the living conditions for Naomi and herself. As Ruth did that, God sent Boaz to notice her! Boaz noticed Ruth *while* she was working! Ruth did not search for Boaz. She was totally focused on her assignment.

Bond with Jesus. Seek His kingdom purposes and plans more than anything else. This is the perfect time to be "souled out" to Jesus. While you're young and single, you won't have to juggle your time and attention between Jesus, a husband, children, and a career. Ask Jesus to give you wisdom to work on you. Ask Jesus, daily, to create in you a clean mind and heart. Take loving care of your house (your spiritual and physical body and your brick-and-mortar home) and car. Go to work and maintain a good name. Model respectable character on your job. Pay your bills on time and pay off unnecessary debt. Cut up overly enticing credit cards. While you're working on you, God will cause your "Boaz" to notice you! Stay focused on and complete the assignments God has given to you.

Younger married women must seek Jesus' closeness, too. Fight against your own crowded daily schedule to get at least fifteen minutes of "quiet time" with Jesus. In those fifteen minutes (in the car, in the bathroom, on the porch), by faith, melt into Jesus' protective arms while "casting all your care upon Him, for He cares for you" (1 Peter 5:7 NKJV). Listen to Him reassure you that He cares for you. Seek His help in working on yourself so you won't be irked by your husband's behaviors. Ask Jesus to keep your mind and wash your heart clean. In the Bible, David asked for a clean heart, and we should do no less. Psalm 51:10 (KJV) says, "Create in me a clean heart, O God; and renew a right spirit within me." Continue praying to keep a clean heart every time you become irritated. Hebrews 10:22 (NKJV) says, "Let us draw near with a true heart in full assurance of faith, having our hearts sprinkled from an evil conscience and our bodies washed with pure water."

Develop your personal relationship with Jesus by confessing to Him that you know you have sinned and made yourself unclean before Him. Tell Him you understand that you deserve death as the punishment and price for your sins. But you know, by faith, He has already paid the price. Tell Him, "Thank You!" Tell Jesus you repent (choose to turn away from self to God) of your lifestyle of selfishness and sin. Confess Him as your Savior and Lord. Tell Him, by faith, you receive the indwelling of the Holy Spirit, and you are saved! Romans 10:9-10 (NKJV) says, "that if you confess with your mouth the Lord Jesus and believe in your heart that God has raised Him from the dead, you will be saved. For with the heart, one believes unto righteousness, and with the mouth confession is made unto salvation." To keep growing in relationship with Jesus, read Scripture daily. That's how you'll get to know Jesus' voice. That's how you'll know what Jesus likes and does not like, what Jesus wants you to do or not do.

By faith, ask the Holy Spirit to help you understand what you read. More importantly, ask the Holy Spirit what to do with what you read; how to apply it to your own life. *Woman up* and ask the Holy Spirit to help you be honest with Him and yourself. Would you benefit from being mentored and "bonus mothered" by Christian women who, as John Piper puts it, "age into a sage?"[25] As you notice the authentic lives of various older Christian women, ask the Holy Spirit to connect you with the *right* older Christian women. Ask Him to surround you with women who will be loving, honest, confidential, available, and dedicated to a mentoring relationship. John 14:26 (NKJV) says, "But the Helper, the Holy Spirit, whom the Father will send in My name, He will teach you all things and bring to your remembrance all things that I said to you."

Seek Sage Guidance from Older Godly Women

Younger women, *woman up* to receive all the wisdom and instructions from wise older women. One Sunday, a couple came to the altar. The young wife was at the end of her rope, so to speak. They came to the altar seeking help from the Lord to save their marriage of over twenty years. The young wife was in tears as she ached with care to hold their marriage together. Knowing my passion for serving women in need, the Lord had me and another wise woman in the right place at the right time. "And we know that all things work together for good to those who love God, to those who are the called according to *His* purpose" (Romans 8:28 NKJV). We listened and empathized. We told her about our experiences and even laughed. We gave her Scriptures that speak to what the Bible says about marriage. We gave the couple tactical biblical strategies for marriage. We prayed with them individually and as a couple, and we exchanged telephone numbers to stay connected.

There is a blessing in staying connected, older woman to younger woman. Pastor Darrell Jackson, Sr. said godly support is available for you "when you realize [you] can't do it on [your] own."[26] I can personally speak to that. Jackie is an older woman in my life who is filled with wisdom and prayer. I don't have to think about doing life on my own because she has been there with me for about twenty-nine years. She and I have prayed and laughed through many tough situations. Momma Pat is also an older woman in my life who is filled with wisdom and prayer. She checks on me, prays for me, and encourages me as I am blessed to watch her walk through life with poise and grace. The blessing of these connections for me encourages me to *woman up*. I get the great privilege of serving as a wise, older woman of prayer to support young women, including Swanzetta, who is my cosmetologist.

Many of us are poised and ready to fill in where necessary. It is our desire and responsibility to support younger women as they grow into Christian womanhood. Godly conversation, prayer, instruction, and correction goes a long way. When instruction is ignored, spiritual growth and transformation are hindered, if not lost altogether. In a time when people are quick to dismiss older people and deem us out of touch or think we have nothing to offer the people of today, we stand ready to fulfill the Titus 2:3-5 mandate. That mandate advises "the older women likewise, that they be reverent in behavior, not slanderers, not given to much wine, teachers of good things—that they admonish the young women to love their husbands, to love their children, to *be* discreet, chaste, homemakers, good, obedient to their own husbands, that the word of God may not be blasphemed" (Titus 2:3-5 NKJV). Younger women have the opportunity to utilize one of God's greatest living resources: a wise, seasoned woman of God! It's our immense pleasure to *woman up* and positively, spiritually influence generations of younger women for ages to come.

Reflection Questions

1. How can you seek out and learn from older, wiser women in your life?

   _____

   _____

   _____

   _____

   _____

2. How have you experienced mentorship and how did it impact your spiritual growth?

   _____

   _____

   _____

   _____

   _____

3. Why is it important to receive correction or instruction from wise, older women?

_____

_____

_____

_____

4. How can you remain open to learning from others, especially older, godly women?

_____

_____

_____

_____

5. What does it mean to you to **woman up** in the context of Christian womanhood and how can this apply to the way you live your everyday life?

_____

_____

_____

_____

Woman Up Prayer

Father, in Jesus' name by the power and the Spirit of the Holy Ghost, it is my desire to see younger women *woman up* Your way. Help us as older women to live and be the examples You've called us to be. Help the younger women long for and seek after us who genuinely "age into a sage." Build bonds between us and younger women that transcend all barriers. Help us to approach our times together based on the words of Hebrews 10:24-25 (NLT) that says, "Let us think of ways to motivate one another to acts of love and good works. And let us not neglect our meeting together, as some people do, but encourage one another, especially now that the day of his return is drawing near." And it *is* so and so it *is* in Jesus' name. *Amen.*

(Write your own prayer on the following page.)

_____

_____

_____

_____

_____

_____

_____

_____

_____

_____

_____

_____

_____

_____

_____

_____

_____

The Charge

The words of a powerfully lined hymn, *A Charge to Keep I Have*, says,

"A charge to keep I have,

A God to glorify,

Who gave His Son my soul to save,

And fit it for, the sky."

A different verse of this same hymn says,

"To serve the present age,

My calling to fulfill,

O, may it all my pow'rs engage

To do my Master's will."

In this present age, in the perilous times we are living in, may we do life God's way. Now, by the power that God has already given each of us as godly women, let us accept and complete this charge as we lift each other up. Older women, mentor and mother younger women. Younger women, seek and receive the wise counsel of older women. Then, serve as an older godly woman in the lives of women younger than you.

I charge each of us to *woman up*!

Notes

Introduction

1. John C. Maxwell and Chris Hodges, *JESUS the HIGH ROAD LEADER: Follow the Path He Wants us to Travel*, (Nashville, TN: Maxwell Leadership, 2024) 14.

2. Merrill C. Tenney and Steven Barabas, Th.D., *Pictorial Bible Dictionary with Topical Index*, (Nashville, TN: The Southwestern Company, 1976) 317.

3. Collins, s.v. "womanly," accessed August 26, 2024, https://www.collinsdictionary.com/dictionary/english/womanly

Tip #1

4. Before I Tell Them by Yolanda Adams (Save the World, 1993) https://www.youtube.com/watch?v=Tq_TXy2Edp8

5. Wayne Grudem. *Systematic Theology: An Introduction to Biblical Doctrine,* (Grand Rapids, MI: Zondervan, 1194) 376.

6. John C. Maxwell, *The 16 Undeniable Laws of Communication,* (Duluth, GA: Maxwell Leadership, 2023) 19.

7. Quoted from Dr. Dharius Daniels in Ministry Mastery Academy.

Tip #2

8. Carol Stine. "Who Was Deborah in the Bible?" Renew.org, Accessed September 3, 2024, https://renew.org/who-was-deborah-in-the-bible/

9. Merrill C. Tenney and Steven Barabas, Th.D., *Pictorial Bible Dictionary with Topical Index (from the Topical Index section),* (Nashville, TN: The Southwestern Company, 1976) 65.

10. "Who Was Anna the Prophetess in the Bible?" Got Questions Ministries, accessed September 12, 2024, [https://www.gotquestions.org/Anna-the-prophetess.html#:~:text=Anna%20is%20mentioned%20in%20the,the%20rest%20of%20her%20life]

Tip #3

11. "What Does the Bible Say About Loyalty?" Got
    Questions Ministries, accessed September 14, 2024,
    [https://www.gotquestions.org/Bible-loyalty.html]

12. Ibid.

13. Biblehub, s.v. "Train", accessed September 14, 2024,
    https://biblehub.com/topical/t/train.htm

14. "Spiritual Leadership in the Home" Focus on the
    Family.com, accessed September 16, 2024,
    https://www.focusonthefamily.com/family-
    qa/spiritual-leadership-in-the-home/

15. Quoted on Maxwell Leadership website, John Maxwell.
    ". . . Everyone deserves to be led well." Accessed
    November 1, 2024,
    https://www.maxwellleadership.com/

Tip #4

16. Blue Letter Bible, s.v. "Discreet", accessed September
    19, 2024, https://www.blueletterbible.org/search/
    Dictionary/viewTopic.cfm?topic=VT0000756

17. Collins, s.v., "Chaste", accessed October 7, 2024,
    https://www.collinsdictionary.com/us/dictionary/englis
    h/chaste#:~:text=adjective,He%20remained%20chaste.

18. Lori Alexander, "Teaching Your Children to Be Chaste", The Transformed Wife. March 31, 2021, https://thetransformedwife.com/teaching-your-children-to-be-chaste-2/

19. Joy Kincaid, "Homemaking: A Biblical Perspective", Artful Homemaking. October 20, 2015, https://www.artfulhomemaking.com/a-biblical-view-of-homemaking/

20. Dr. J. Vernon McGee, "Titus 2:1-5", Blue Letter Bible. Accessed October 10, 2024, https://www.blueletterbible.org/audio_video/popPlayer.cfm?id=8829&rel=mcgee_j_vernon/english/tts

21. Ibid.

22. Bugs Bunny, "Them's fightin' words!' https://www.youtube.com/watch?v=2nTeQS09dDs

23. "What Is Blasphemy?", Got Questions Ministries, accessed October 14, 2024, [https://www.gotquestions.org/blasphemy-blaspheme.html]

24. William MacDonald, *Believer's Bible Commentary: A Complete Bible Commentary in One Volume.* (Nashville, TN: Thomas Nelson Publishers, 1995), 2139.

Tip #5

25. John Piper, *When I Don't Desire God*, (Wheaton, IL: Crossway, 2004), 109-110.

26. Pastor Darrell Jackson, Sr. Sermon: *From Despair to Joy*. https://bwcar.org/episode/from-despair-to-joy-audio/

About the Author

While many women seek fortune and fame, she's on a mission to transform hearts and minds for the kingdom of God. As a retired educator/literacy coach and certified John Maxwell Leadership coach, speaker and trainer, Catherine S. Hamilton knows firsthand that true fulfillment only comes from encouraging and empowering others while living an authentic lifestyle that glorifies God. Intentional about knowing God deeper—and making Him known to others—Catherine is devoted to the expository teaching of the Word of God to women of all ages and backgrounds.

An ordained elder with a Master of Arts Degree in Bible Exposition from Columbia International University, Catherine strives to deposit practical instructions and a plethora of Scriptures into every person she meets. In addition to her Bachelor of Arts in Early Childhood Education and Master of Education Degrees from the University of South Carolina-Aiken, Catherine also attained National Board Certification in Literacy: Reading-Language Arts/Early and Middle Childhood.

In her debut book, *Woman Up! Five Tips for Godly Women,* Catherine takes readers on a journey to be free in their minds and hearts unapologetically. As a beacon of hope for Christian women who long to pour into generations of younger women through sound doctrine, Catherine encourages younger women to seek wisdom, support and life strategies from sage women who are committed to walking alongside them in every facet of life. Having served in ministry since adolescence, Catherine is intentional about living the Word of God out loud.

In addition to her new book, Catherine spends her time pouring into others through her service on prayer conference calls and masterminds. Catherine resides in Aiken, South Carolina with her husband, Deacon Gene E. Hamilton, and is the proud mother of two adult children: Maresha and Edwin. For more information, coaching, or speaking engagements, email cat2hamilton@aol.com or call 803.645.0278.